Ride the Black Hills

By Cynthia Lueck Sowden

© 2016, Cynthia Lueck Sowden

Cover Design: Lisa Marek, Fat Cat Art Studio

Cover Photo: Riding through the Needles Tunnel

First Edition

ISBN: 0692750851

ISBN-13: 978-0692750858

Table of Contents

*To Karen Rusert at the Harley-Davidson Shop of
Winona, Minnesota, who encouraged me to write this book.*

Introduction

"God," said the farmer. "You guys must be as tough as nails."

We had stopped in Faith, South Dakota, for an unplanned fuel stop. The temperature was in the mid-forties, and the wind was howling straight out of the west, down US 212 and into our faces. Gusts from the north snatched and grabbed for my helmet, and I put one hand up to hold it place. I thought, crazily, that I might end up with whiplash. Cold air swirled inside it and around my head, and I wondered (not for the first time) why God had seen fit to equip me with thin, fine hair.

Ralph filled the Victory's tank. We had left Gettysburg on the Missouri River with a full tank and had traveled only 92 miles; running against the wind had dwindled our gas supply to just one gallon.

This wouldn't be the last time someone asked us if we were cold, or crazy, or both. A guy in Spearfish blamed us for bringing bad weather. A few people apologized for the weather, adding helpfully, "It was in the seventies last week."

Welcome to South Dakota!

We rode the Black Hills the second week of May, a chancy time of year in that part of the world. We wanted to be able to experience the roads without crowds of summer tourists; to see Sturgis before the big rally in August. We had some dicey moments along the way, but persevered. This book is the result.

Get out and Ride the Black Hills!
Cynthia Lueck Sowden
July 2016

P.S.: We traveled to the Black Hills via US 212. If you're headed that way, stop in at Bob's Resort in Gettysburg. It's ten miles west of town on the Missouri River. The place is a former state park and the view is gorgeous. If you're planning a stay, make reservations well in advance; the Oahe Reservoir is a popular fishing hole. The restaurant opens daily at 5 p.m., and it serves some of the best steaks ever cut from a cow. Ralph's was two inches thick!

Chapter 1

Before You Go

South Dakota has its own rules and regulations for motorcycles, and its own peculiar climate. It's good to know a little about these topics before you put up your kickstand.

South Dakota Motorcycle Laws

DOT-Approved Helmets

Helmets are a must for anyone under the age of 18. High gusts of wind have been known to cause freak accidents in valleys and at the tops of hills. You may want to consider wearing yours.

Handlebar Height

Restrictions on handlebar height were lifted July 1, 2015.

Eye Protection

Some form of eye protection is required, whether it's a pair of safety goggles, a windshield or a full-face helmet. If you're going to ride at night, make sure your eye protection is not tinted or shaded, and does not reduce light transmission to a level below 35 percent.

Blue Dot Taillight

Your bike can have a blue light as part of your rear taillight. Your red light must be visible for at least 500 feet.

Muffler

South Dakotans don't like noise in "them thar hills". Excessive or unusual noise could get you a ticket.

Insurance

It never hurts to make sure your insurance coverage is up to date. South Dakota requires compulsory liability insurance, with minimum limits of 25/50/25.

Riding Two Abreast

Two bikers can ride side-by-side in the same lane in the Mount Rushmore State, but more than two is a misdemeanor offense.

Passing in the Same Lane

It's a no-no.

Using the Full Lane

Motorcyclists have full use of the lane they ride in. It's against the law for another motor vehicle to deprive you of full use of the lane.

Lane Splitting

Guess you'll have to go to Great Britain. It's illegal in South Dakota, and it's a misdemeanor offense if you're caught.

Speed Limits

Interstate Highways	75 mph
Secondary Highways	65 mph
Residential and Business Areas	25 mph
Near Schools	15 mph

Posted speeds vary considerably on the tight curves and winding roads of the Black Hills. Stick to the suggested speed limits and you'll live to ride another day.

Wyoming Motorcycle Laws

Because this book also takes you to Wyoming, here's a quick review of motorcycle laws in the Cowboy State.

Helmets
Helmets are required for riders under 18 years of age.

Using the Full Lane
Motorcyclists have full use of the lane they ride in. It's against the law for another motor vehicle to deprive you of full use of the lane.

Riding Three Abreast
It's not allowed, but you can ride two abreast.

Handlebar Height
Sorry, ape hangers are not allowed if they extend above shoulder height.

Passing in the Same Lane
You can pass another motorcycle in the same lane, but no other vehicles. You must match the speed of the motorcycle you're over-taking before you pass it.

Speed Limits
Interstate Highways ....75 mph

Secondary Highways....................................65 mph

Residential and Business Areas ....30 mph

Near Schools ....20 mph

South Dakota Weather

You definitely want to pay attention to the weather in South Dakota. With the high plains to the west of the Black Hills and the prairie to the east, weather can change quickly.

Daily high temperatures run in the high 60s to high 70s in May and June. July and August usually come with temps in the 80s. In September and October, average temperatures slowly drop back to the 60s. Night-time lows in the Black Hills during motorcycle season are generally in the 50s. Pack some warm layers! Leather chaps can provide welcome warmth in the morning.

Those are averages, however. The Black Hills can be a land of extremes. On January 22, 1943, the temperature in Spearfish was recorded at -4 at 7:32 a.m. In two minutes, it rose to 45 degrees! It crept up to 54 two hours later, then plunged back to -4 in 27 minutes. Although you probably won't encounter that kind of numbing cold during motorcycle season, it's an illustration of how quickly things can change.

May is the month that brings the most precipitation to the Black Hills. Whatever month you visit, be sure to pack your rain gear. Thunderstorms and hail can be a daily threat throughout the summer.

Snow is always a possibility during "shoulder months" of May and September, especially in the higher elevations. If you do encounter snow during a ride, consider this advice from the Wyoming Department of Transportation:

If the road is slippery, the grip your tires have is reduced. Therefore, drive slower than you would on a dry road. When driving on:

Wet road   Reduce speed by at least 5-10 mph.

Packed snow   Reduce speed by at least half.

Ice   Reduce speed to a crawl.

Be on the lookout for Buffalo and other wildlife!

It's very windy in South Dakota. Sudden downdrafts and updrafts can add an exciting new dimension to the curves and switchbacks in the mountains. We encountered 30 mph straight-line winds with gusts of up to 50 mph on our way from Belle Fourche to Devils Tower. When we parked our bike at the tower, Ralph stuck his helmet on the backrest of the seat. When we returned after a hike, it had blown off and was rolling around the parking lot. A young man who had just parked next to us said he had visited Dinosaur Park near Rapid City and his Harley blew over. Stay alert and keep the shiny side up!

Wildlife

Locals caution against night riding in the Black Hills because of the area's abundance of wildlife. One-third of traffic accidents in South Dakota are caused by wildlife. Between July 1, 2011 and June 30, 2012, State Farm Insurance reported 8,863 deer-related accidents in South Dakota. Be on the lookout for animals, especially during early morning and early evening hours.

Bison, pronghorn, bighorn sheep, mountain goats, burros, coyotes, falcons, mule deer, mountain lions, and bobcats are scattered throughout the region. White-tailed deer are very prevalent; it's not uncommon to round a curve and have four or five leap away from you, their tails a white flag.

If you come across a herd of buffalo blocking the road, pull over and wait, especially in Custer State Park. Keep a safe distance; signs throughout the area warn against approaching these unpredictable critters. Don't challenge them or rev your engine to scare them off. They don't take kindly to challenges, and more than one biker has reported that they charge bikes with loud pipes. Whatever you do, don't get off your bike to take a selfie with a bison. It's not unusual for area newscasts to report on the hospitalization or death of a

Sometimes, a guardrail is all that's between you and the canyon below.

Road crews get ready for the summer tourist season.

tourist who stood next to a buffalo for a photo. If you do tangle with a buffalo, don't blame it on the beast. As Lora Martin, supervisor of the Hill City Visitor Information Center, said, "Back East, they'd destroy the buffalo. Out here, people say, 'You've been warned', and the buffalo lives."

The Roads

The roads in the Black Hills are some of the best we've ridden. For the most part, the pavement is smooth, with few potholes, and few bumps. Hats off to South Dakota for a beautiful maintenance job throughout the state!

Whether you're fairly new to riding or highly experienced, the roads in the Black Hills have much to offer, including hairpin turns, sharp and shallow curves, inclines and declines, twisties, pigtail bridges, and narrow or non-existent road shoulders. There are breath-taking overlooks where you can stop and take pictures and places where you'll hold your breath because there is nothing but a guardrail between you and the canyon below.

Turns and speed limits are clearly marked.

The turns and curves are well marked, and the speed limits posted along some of the twistier roads such as the Needles Highway and Iron Mountain Road are realistic. Some places specifically warn motorcyclists to take caution. If you follow the directions, keep your speed at or just slightly below the posted limit, and your eyes on the road, you should be able to navigate through this beautiful back country without too many problems.

Watch out for gravel near intersections with unpaved roads or highways. And keep an eye out for motorists who are afraid to drive tight curves or brake in the middle of them.

National Parks Pass

You may want to consider obtaining a national parks pass before you leave home. It's $80 per year, and it admits you to all National Parks in the U.S., including Devil's Tower. If you're currently serving in the military, passes are free. If you're 62 or older, you can buy a lifetime pass for a flat $10. With the pass, you don't have to go through the hassle of carrying cash to enter a park, and the rangers treat you like royalty when they give tours.

A Word About the Sturgis Rally

Attending the annual motorcycle rally in Sturgis is on many a motorcyclist's list. It is one big, week-long biker party.

If you plan to attend, don't wait to book a place to stay. Although the Black Hills have a plentiful number of hotels, motels, and campsites, the longer you wait, the more you'll pay. According to Myrick Robbins, executive director of the Sturgis Motorcycle Museum and Hall of Fame, area hoteliers are not shy about charging up to three times their normal rate during Rally week; it's a matter of supply and demand. Call 866-STURGIS.

If you plan to camp, research the camps. Some party into the wee hours and others are more sedate. If you want to get a good night's sleep, avoid the party camp. Some Sturgis residents rent their front yards to campers; others rent their homes. Wherever you stay, the people of Sturgis ask that you please show respect.

Remember that some Sturgis residents have small children. Try to avoid doing something you'd have trouble explaining to a six-year-old – or to your mother.

We talked to the mother of a woman who lives in Sturgis. Her daughter stayed home for the 75th Rally and her mother asked what it was like. Replied the daughter, "Imagine everyone in town mowing their lawns continuously from dawn until dark, and then the neighbors fighting over the back fence until morning, when they start the lawn mowers again."

Attend to your personal safety as well. The South Dakota Department of Public Safety quite plainly states, "Every year people die at the Rally, many due to alcohol-related crashes. Stay sober and stay safe." In 2015 during the 75th Motorcycle Rally, 13 motorcyclists died and 152 were injured. Be careful out there!

Sturgis veterans warn to be on the lookout for other riders. Human beings are as unpredictable as buffalo. When they're on their bikes, they may make sudden turns or stops without warning. They may get impatient and cross the center line on a curve. Some are new riders who don't know about staggered riding when they're in a group and will ride in the center of the lane. The roads will be packed during the rally. Keep a safe distance between your bike and others' and be ready to go slow and stop often. Take your turn at the tunnels. And, beautiful as the scenery is, pay attention to the road!

Veteran riders say traffic increases as the day warms up; the best time to ride is early morning. Rally accidents typically start to occur midday.

The Department of Public Safety also suggests investing in a motorcycle lock and locking saddlebags. As in any crowd, there are some people who will prey on the unsuspecting.

Black Hills weather is unpredictable. Severe thunderstorms, large hail, strong downburst winds, and flash flooding may occur during the rally. The City of Sturgis will sound its outdoor warning sirens for tornadoes only.

Each year, the Sturgis Motorcycle Rally publishes a guide that tells you everything about the event, including the "Rally Zones", camping spots, the safest routes to take when you've been drinking (stay the hell away from me!), and shortcuts in and around Sturgis so you don't spend all your time in traffic. You can access it online and download it to your computer or iPad. There's a cost involved, but the information in the guide will not only give you an idea of what to expect at the rally, it could save your life! Go to **http://www.sturgismotorcyclerally.com/shop-link/rally-guide-book.**

Lower Limits

Beginning with the 2016 Rally, the State of South Dakota lowers the speed limits during Rally Week. The lower limits begin on the Thursday before the rally and continue through the last Sunday of the rally. During the eleven days of the rally, the speed limit on I90 between Sturgis and Rapid City is 65 mph. A segment of SD 34 east of Blanche Street in Sturgis is lowered to 35 mph for nearly four miles, and a two-mile stretch north of the Blanche/SD 34 intersection is lowered to 45 mph. The 45-mph zone on SD 79 runs from Sturgis to the Iron Horse Campground.

Devils Tower is an awe-inspiring sight even from afar.

Chapter 2

The Rides

When it comes to motorcycling, the Black Hills has it all: Long, sweeping curves, tight little mountainside twisties, pigtail bridges, and tunnels, all flanked by some of the most beautiful scenery on earth. You'll ride through pine forests and wide-open spaces, inhale fresh mountain air, and revel in it all.

The rides in this section are in the order we took them. Some are quite short, but challenging. Most have been rated in terms of difficulty by A.B.A.T.E. of South Dakota. The rides range from black (easy) to yellow (difficult). You can get a free copy of A.B.A.T.E.'s skill-rated map from **www.travelsouthdakota.com**. Go to the "Request a Vacation Guide" page and scroll down to the button for the motorcycle packet, which also includes an official South Dakota road map.

Belle Fourche, South Dakota to Devils Tower, Wyoming

53 miles via SD 14 and WY 24

A.B.A.T.E. Skill Level: Blue (moderate)

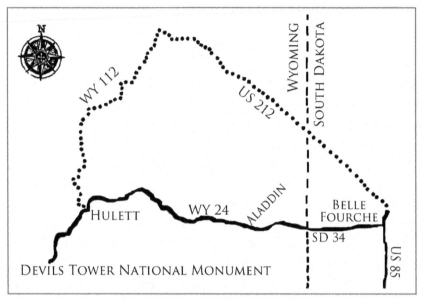

Belle Fourche to Devils Tower via US 34/WY 24. An alternative route takes you up US 212 to WY 112 and down to the monument.

Belle Fourche is where John Wayne and a bunch of little boys took their herd to market in "The Cowboys". (It's still a big livestock market.) The city stands at the confluence of the Belle Fourche and Redwater Rivers and is the geographical center of the United States. A little museum in town commemorates this with flags and a compass rose. We thought about seeking out the official location, but decided against it when a convenience store clerk told us it was "twenty miles out of town in some guy's field." The weather was just too damn cold.

After thawing out from our morning ride from Gettysburg, we wound our way through Belle Fourche to US 85, which brought us to US 34 near the Belle Fourche Country Club. We took the cloverleaf and headed west.

Like Gaston in Disney's "Beauty and the Beast", Hulett uses antlers in all of its decorating.

US 34, as it leaves Belle Fourche, is a good two-lane highway that gently curves through the land. In spring, the earth is bright green. Streams cut through the rounded buttes; cottonwood trees trace the waters' route. We passed over bridges that had no water under them; those low spots must fill mighty fast during a storm!

The wind battered us as we rolled along beside hayfields and pastures filled with Black Angus cattle. Though they're nowhere near as numerous as the buffalo once were, these shiny black beasts dot many a hillside in South Dakota. Beef is what's for dinner throughout the state.

As the highway crosses the South Dakota line, its name changes to WY 24. The terrain becomes more rugged. Past Aladdin (a town so small — 50 people — you wonder why Wyoming bothered to post a sign), it begins a nine-mile series of tight, climbing curves. Devils Tower was a gray, misty sentinel, barely visible through as we approached the summit. We then encountered some sweepers before hitting a 9 percent downgrade that leads to seven more miles of tight curves. The curves are well marked. If you adhere to the suggested speed limit, you should have no trouble making your way through this territory.

The Belle Fourche River — its name is French for "beautiful fork" — suddenly reappears as you near the city of Hulett. A tributary of the Cheyenne River, it's part of the Mississippi River watershed system. The road, meanwhile, continues to curve and climb and nearly doubles back on itself just before you roll across a bridge over the Belle Fourche and into Hulett, tucked under the red rim rocks of the Bear Lodge Mountains.

Hulett is a ranching community, and has a real Old West feel. Lewis Hulett established a general store there in 1866 to cater to timber cutters in the area who supplied materials for gold prospectors in the Black Hills. Its proximity to Devils Tower and Sturgis brings thousands of tourists and bikers through town each year. Deer and elk antlers are a popular decoration for businesses along Main Street.

As Hwy. 24 pulls you through town, it connects with WY 112, part of the alternate route from Belle Fourche shown on the map. It crosses the Belle Fourche River again and makes a long, curving run to Devils Tower. The river valley is flat, which makes the tower all the more impressive. Take a right at WY 110/Crook County 174 and follow it past the Devils Tower KOA to the national monument's visitor center.

Devils Tower is the U.S.' first national monument, designated by President Theodore Roosevelt in 1906. It rises 1,267 feet above the Belle Fourche River. Geologist believe that the tower, once thought to be an extinct volcano, is a stock, a small body of magma that formed underground and was exposed by erosion. It acquired the Devils Tower name in 1875 when Lieutenant Colonel Richard

Dodge escorted a geological expedition through the Black Hills in search of gold. The Indian words for "Bear Lodge" were misinterpreted as "Bad God's Tower", and the name stuck.

The monument is sacred ground to more than 20 Native American tribes. In 2014, the Oglala Sioux filed a proposal with the U.S. Board on Geographic names to change the name back to Bear Lodge. In 2015, Wyoming Senator Mike Enzi and Representative Cynthia Lummis introduced bills in Congress to retain the Devils Tower moniker. It may take years to decide the issue.

The entry fee for motorcycles is $5 per person. The parking lot can be quite crowded during the summer, especially between the hours of 11 a.m. and 2 p.m. There is additional parking near the picnic area, which affords a fantastic view of the tower. Lines to get into the site stretch for miles during Sturgis week and the park service runs a shuttle for owners of long vehicles that week.

Take a break from riding and stretch your legs with a hike on the 1.3-mile path around the base of the tower. It's paved, and it's a relatively easy walk. Take water with you – temperatures next to the tower can easily reach 100 degrees.

The flat areas surrounding the tower are pock-marked with prairie dog towns. Although they're cute and furry, the National Park Service discourages feeding them. They like to bite, and they carry bubonic plague.

Stop into the Visitor Center and learn about the geology and history of the place where "Close Encounters of the Third Kind" was filmed. The center also has a book store and some souvenirs.

The Devils Tower Trading Post outside the main entrance also has souvenirs. You can pick up a patch for your jacket there and sample some huckleberry ice cream, a local flavor favorite.

The Legend

The Legend of the Devils Tower

The Lakota and the Cheyenne called it "Bear Lodge;" the Arapaho, "Bear's Tipi"; the Crow, "Bear's Home"; the Assiniboine, "Place Where Bears Live"; the Mandan, "Bear's Hat"; and the Kiowa, "Rock Tree." All share a similar story about the place known as Devils Tower.

A group of Indians camped beside the river. Bears were numerous in the area. Seven little girls were playing at a distance from the encampment when a bear (some say it was the girls' brother) started to chase them. They climbed up on a rock and pleaded with the rock to save them. The rock rose high up into the sky. The bear tried to climb the rock. It dug its claws in deep, but couldn't get a grip. The rock continued to grow and pushed the girls into the sky, where they remain as the Seven Sisters (Pleiades) constellation.

It's easy to see where the bear sharpened its claws.

Devils Tower, Wyoming to Spearfish, South Dakota

60 miles via US 14/Old US 14

A.B.A.T.E. Skill Level: Blue (moderate)

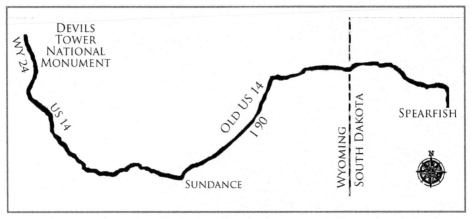

Old US 14 parallels I 90.

After a brief lunch of sausage, cheese, and crackers in the Devils Tower picnic area, we watched the prairie dogs pop up from their burrows and walked over to view the Circle of Sacred Smoke sculpture by Japanese artist Junkuy Moto. Placed to frame the tower, it represents the first puff of smoke from a peace pipe. Moto has similar installations at the Vatican and Bodh Gaya, India, and plans to have one at Ground Zero in New York. All are intended to promote peace.

We saddled up once more and wound our way back along Hwy. 110 to WY 24, where we took a right and headed south toward Sundance. The road curved easily past ranches on our right and pine forests on our left.

Two miles from the monument entrance, there's a pullout on the left side of the road (right, if you're coming from the opposite direction) where you can take another look at Devils Tower. The Tower View Café is also there, and little further from the road, Devils Tower Tipi Camping offers a chance to camp under the stars in a tipi. The tipis accommodate four to six people, but the cold wind reminded me this was not the kind of day I wanted to try this mode of lodging.

The road continues its lazy meander to US 14. Take a left and head toward Sundance at Carlile Junction. US 14 cuts through country that becomes increasingly mountainous as you head southeast. The curves and climbs are pleasant, but not challenging.

You have a choice at Sundance: You can jump on I 90 and ride the freeway to Spearfish, or you can take old US 14 out of Sundance. It parallels the freeway. Although you may have to make an occasional stop for a stray cow, it's almost as fast, and can be a good alternative route during Sturgis week.

Sundance got its start in 1879, when Albert Hoge, a Prussian immigrant, staked his claim. At his insistence, the town was named after the sun dance ceremony performed by many Plains cultures. We detoured into Sundance to see if we could find the statue of the Sundance Kid, who was a real person.

Henry Longabaugh was arrested for stealing a horse and spent 18 months in the Sundance jail. His jail term earned him the "Sundance Kid" nickname. In due time, he hooked up with Butch Cassidy and the two of them began a life of robbing banks and trains. The Kid's statue is next to the Crook County Museum at 309 Cleveland St. Unfortunately, we wheeled through town on Main Street and missed it. Having once gone on a fruitless search for Standin' on the Corner Park in Winslow, Arizona, we didn't pursue the Sundance Kid with any real vigor. The museum is open 8 a.m. to 5 p.m. Monday through Friday during June, July and August. It closes an hour earlier during the off season.

We stayed on Old US 14 when we left town. The freeway was never out of sight, although the old road did make an occasional swing away from the big concrete ribbons of the interstate.

The Vore Buffalo Jump is about halfway between Sundance and Spearfish, before you reach Beulah, Wyoming. It was discovered on the Vore family's ranch in the early 1970s when surveys were conducted prior to the construction of I 90. The jump is a sinkhole that was used at least twenty times between 1550 and 1800 by Native American tribes who herded and pushed bison off the edge of the sinkhole. Archeologists have excavated 22 levels at the site, revealing not only the bones of buffalo, but various implements from stone tools to metal trade knives. As more tribes acquired horses, the practice of chasing bison off a cliff became extinct. The Vore Buffalo Jump is open June 1 through Labor Day. Admission is $7 per person.

We sped along Old 14, stopping occasionally as a school bus dropped kids off along the way. It was a chilly May day, and some of the kids wore winter jackets, cowboy boots and Stetsons. Just before we reached Spearfish, Old 14 ducked under a viaduct and we made a slower entrance into town.

Spearfish Canyon Scenic Byway

20 miles via US 14A

A.B.A.T.E. Skill Level: Red (somewhat challenging)

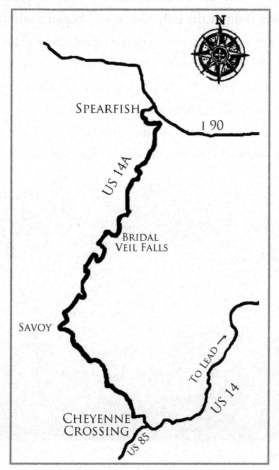

The Scenic Byway climbs nearly 2,000 feet from Spearfish to Cheyenne Crossing.

Weather conditions may vary. That warning is posted on the Spearfish Canyon Foundation website. It should be posted at each end of the Spearfish Canyon Scenic Byway!

The sky was overcast. The temperature in downtown Spearfish was 48 degrees, but the wind wasn't blowing as hard as it did the previous day.

There was nothing on our cell phones' radar that indicated any major weather events were likely to occur.

After filling up, we drove south down Main Street to where it touches US 14A. We took a right at the golf course and began a winding drive to Cheyenne Crossing, a convenience store/restaurant that marks the end of the scenic byway. We crossed Spearfish Creek, and the stream stayed to our left for most of the ride. The creek was high, thanks to recent snowmelt, and had a beautiful aquamarine blue color that seems to be peculiar to the Black Hills. Birches and other deciduous trees splashed bright green leaves against the almost black needles of the Ponderosa pines.

Main Street, Spearfish

The road was nicely paved, with an occasional passing lane added to make the trip smoother. We pretty much had the road to ourselves, so it didn't matter. The speed limit was 35 mph. We began a series of S-curves as the road began to climb. Limestone walls a thousand feet high rose above us and shielded us from the wind. Signs warned of falling rock. A light mist was in the air, but the road remained dry. The road made a couple of sharp turns and we could see the mist at the tops of the mountains.

We pulled over at Bridal Veil Falls, dismounted, and crossed the road for a better look. The falls were indeed a thin veil of water sliding down the rocks to the creek below. It was hard to believe that Spearfish Creek was once on the same level as the falls. A young woman got out of her car to take pictures and we decided it was time to move on.

Spearfish Canyon's limestone palisades provided great wind protection.

The mist turned to rain as the road began climbing, still no cause for concern. The rain began to fall more heavily as we passed by the old Homestake Mining hydro plant at Maurice. Built in 1917, it provided power for gold mining operations for nearly 100 years.

As the road led us to higher elevations, the rain turned… white. Some areas were more sheltered, and the weather eased up a bit. Then the hills ahead of us slowly disappeared behind a gray veil as the snow increased and Savoy came into view. Savoy consists of little more than an intersection. Roughlock Falls, The Latchstring Inn Restaurant, and the Spearfish Canyon Resort stare across the road at each other. Lawrence County Rd. 222 leads you to Roughlock Falls and the "Dances With Wolves" winter filming site. In a somewhat spooky coincidence, the theme from the movie began playing over and over in my head. We remained on US 14.

As Ralph emailed to his mother that evening, "A gentle mist was falling as we passed Bridal Veil Falls and as we climbed higher, slush started building up on the windshield. Then you could see it coating the trees. Then the ground. Then the highway."

I began to feel uncomfortable as the slush started to build on the road. We're both experienced winter drivers, but as Ralph said, "Here we are driving in the snow on a curvy mountain road on a bike with tires that have no business riding on it."

Bridal Veil Falls is a popular place to pull over and regard nature.

Spearfish Creek crossed over to the right side of the road as we continued to climb toward Elmore. It foamed over little rapids and continued its downhill rush. Ralph maintained his cool and a steady speed, easing up on the throttle when he felt the Victory slide. We passed by several lovely-looking log homes, but all our attention was on the road before us.

A sharp turn to the left brought us into Cheyenne Crossing. A former stagecoach stop established in 1878, Cheyenne Crossing serves a similar purpose today. It's a convenience store, restaurant, and three-room lodge. Locals recommend the food, which includes Indian frybread. The lights were on in the restaurant, and a cup of coffee sounded inviting, but we kept on. I'm sure the folks inside wondered who was out riding a motorcycle on such a lousy day.

We took a right at the junction with US 85 and headed toward Newcastle.

Cheyenne Crossing to Newcastle, Wyoming

43 miles via US 85

A.B.A.T.E. Skill Level: Red (somewhat challenging) to Four Corners, then Blue (moderate) to Newcastle

The snow seemed to abate a little as we followed 85 southwest. Spearfish Creek was once again on our left. We passed by Hellsgate

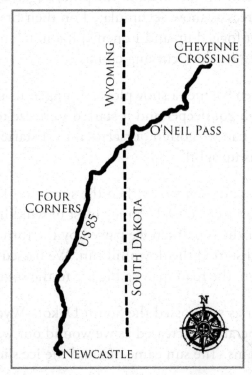

US 85 takes you up 6,683 feet above sea level, then sets you down in Wyoming.

Gulch and Deadhorse Gulch. The crust of ice on the fairing became thicker. Snowflakes began to fly faster and heavier. Patches of snow built up on the hillsides. I wondered how long it had been snowing in this area.

Ralph raised his visor to peer around and over the ice-encrusted windshield. The snow flew between his glasses and his eyes, and it stung. His hands, though gloved, were cold but he didn't dare take them off the grips.

The mountains ahead of us were gray forms in the distance. The slush began to build up on the road, making driving more difficult. It hissed under the tires. I sat still as could be on the back of the bike, trying to avoid doing anything that might send us sledding into the ditch.

The road hugged the banks of Spearfish Creek, and we clung to the curves as it followed the bends in the stream. The pines began to look like Christmas card trees as snow accumulated on their branches. The visor on my helmet fogged up and I opened it a notch to clear it. The road continued its slow, curving climb.

We became concerned when we met a snowplow coming at us in the opposite lane. The slush got deeper and it started to freeze to the outside of my visor. What had we gotten ourselves into? I started praying, "Oh God, keep us upright!"

Another plow came along, and then we reached the summit: O'Neil Pass, elevation 6,683 feet above sea level. An icy blast of wind hit us broadside as we drove over the top. Then we passed by the turnout, which we couldn't see, and started the downhill run. We passed the Trailshead Lodge just before the road made a big arc to the south.

The weather began to clear as we crossed the South Dakota-Wyoming border. The air temperature increased as we wound our way down through the mountains. The sun came out and the ice slid off of the windshield. By the time we reached Buckhorn, the snowstorm had already become a bad memory.

The road made one last big turn and we reached the flatlands. Four Corners soon came into view. An unincorporated town at the intersection of US 85 and WY 585, it was once a stagecoach stop between the Union Pacific Railroad and the goldfields of Deadwood.

Visibility went down rapidly when slush turned to ice on the windshield.

US 85 snaked between Sweetwater Mountain and Mt. Pisgah and some lower hills before leading us into Newcastle.

Newcastle is a player in Wyoming's coal and petroleum industry. It's named after Newcastle-Upon-Tyne, England, another coal-mining town. An oil refinery occupies a large piece of land along Main Street; it produces 14,000 barrels per day. Pumpjacks are scattered outside the town like lost members of a herd of rocking horses.

It had taken us three hours to travel a distance that can normally be covered in an hour and a half. It was lunch time and we were in sore need of some hot food. We rolled up to Donna's Main Street Diner.

Donna herself greeted us at the door, seated us and poured some much-needed hot coffee. "Regulars" came and went as we slowly thawed out. No one paid any attention to us; bikers are welcome, and the restaurant sees its share of them during the Sturgis rally. The long and narrow diner's décor featured a jackalope and a singing deer on one wall and photographs of Wyoming scenery on the other.

If the décor was corny, the food was anything but. Donna talked Ralph into having the day's special, a Monte Cristo sandwich –

Snow began to pile up on and along the road.

ham, turkey and Swiss cheese dipped in egg batter and fried. The cheddar-broccoli soup sounded a little heavy to me, so I opted for an egg salad sandwich, which was lightly flavored with fresh dill.

Donna is the type of woman who loves to feed people, and an expert salesperson. We found we couldn't leave without trying her fresh peach cobbler.

Newcastle to Custer, South Dakota, with a loop to Hot Springs

159 miles via US 16, SD 89. US 385 and SD 87

A.B.A.T.E. Skill Level: Hwys. 16, 89, and 385, Red (somewhat challenging); Hwy. 87, Orange (somewhat difficult); Hwy. 18, Blue (moderate)

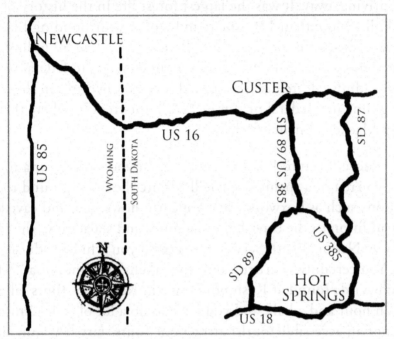

The ride from Newcastle back to the Black Hills makes an interesting afternoon.

US 16 leaving Newcastle is a smooth, two-lane road. It curves gently southeast toward the Black Hills, and is lined with pine trees and ranches. The land is wide and expansive, with small hills and tablelands in the not-too-far distance. There are occasional pull-outs for semis as the road begins a slow climb. The southern end of the Black Hills range beckons you as you hum along, seemingly just out of reach.

The hills begin to close in on you as you cross the Wyoming-South Dakota line. US 16 takes on the additional name of Mt. Rushmore Road. The curves become more numerous as you travel between and though the hills.

The highway becomes twistier as you enter Jewel Cave National Monument. Along the way, you'll see the scars of a forest fire that occurred in 2000. Janice Stevenson of Newcastle stopped to urinate along the road. She lit a cigarette, then tossed it and watched it burn before driving away. It was the largest forest fire in the history of the Black Hills. More than 130 square miles of the surrounding Black Hills were burned in the Jasper fire. It cost more than $9 million to fight the fire, which caused $42 million in damages to federal property. The admitted firebug (she started several other fires in the area) is doing time in a federal prison in Texas. The trees lie where they fell, like blackened matchsticks.

If you've never been to Jewel Cave, I suggest you stop in for a tour. Even if you're not a spelunker, you'll admire the underground rock formations such as boxwork, cave popcorn, flowstone, and cave bacon in addition to the expected stalagmites and stalactites. The tours are run by National Park Service rangers, so you'll find it educational. You certainly won't run into the "aliens", ziplines or a "7-D" interactive ride found at Rushmore Cave in Keystone! Tours take about an hour and a half, and you have to do a lot of stair-climbing; this is not an accessible tourist attraction! Tours start at 9 a.m. and tickets are sold on a first-come, first-served basis.

Hwy. 16 curves on past the Jewel Cave Visitor Center, leading past more downed trees. It straightens out after a few miles, then dips southeast again toward Custer. On the way into town, you'll pass the National Museum of Woodcarving, a good place to visit if the weather is too inclement to ride. The carvings are phenomenal and many one-of-a-kind pieces are for sale. The museum is open from May 1 to October 20. Summer hours are 9 a.m. to 7 p.m.; otherwise, you can visit between the hours of 9 a.m. and 5 p.m.

While you're still in the outskirts of Custer, you'll come up to US 385, also known as Centennial Road and SD 89. Take a right and head south. The highway has many long curves and it takes you past

Custer County Airport; the Newberg Company lumber mill, which has a conical, rusty wood kiln on its property; and a wide spot in the road called Sanator, then makes a relatively straight run through the town of Pringle.

The remains of the Jasper forest fire that occurred in 2000.

You wouldn't think a little place like Pringle would have any notoriety attached to it, but it does. About fifteen miles southwest of town is a compound of the Fundamentalist Church of Jesus Christ of the Latter-Day Saints, an offshoot of the Mormon Church, whose leader is in prison for marrying several under-age girls. The compound is 'way off the beaten track, has a guard tower, and it's probably not worth the effort to go see it, but it could make for interesting conversation at the Hitchrail Bar and Restaurant. It's the only business in town and reportedly serves half-pound burgers.

When you drive past Pringle, US 385 and SD 89 split; stay on SD 89. The road curls around pine-covered hills as you head southwest. The trees become sparser, and soon you're riding through rolling grasslands and cultivated fields of row crops.

Hot Springs' historic buildings include its courthouse and railway station.

At Minnekahta Junction – it's marked – take a left onto US 18. This is the "Blue" (moderate) part of the ride. The highway bends lazily past farms and ranches, then re-enters hill country just before reaching Hot Springs.

Hot Springs' original name was minnekahta (warm waters). The warm mineral waters were a bone of contention between the Cheyenne and the Lakota for decades. The tribes felt the warm waters had curative powers and would come to the area for healing.

When you're in Hot Springs, take the opportunity to visit the Mammoth Site. Several signs point the way to the museum, so it's easy to find. The site was discovered in 1974, when construction crews preparing the ground for a housing development found the fossilized bones of 26,000-year-old woolly and Columbian mammoths. Sixty-one mammoths have been uncovered, in addition to wolves, a short-faced bear, fish, a camel, and other fossils. The museum was built over the site, so you see the bones as if you're on an archeological dig. The Mammoth Site is open from 8 a.m. to 8 p.m. May 14-August 14, 8 a.m. to 6 p.m. through the end of August, and 9 a.m. to 5 p.m. after Labor Day.

To get to US 385, follow US 18 (also known as University Avenue) into Hot Springs all the way to Chicago Street, then turn left. In a block, you'll make another left onto Jennings Avenue. Take a right at the end of the block onto River Street. The Fall River runs alongside the street as you cruise through the older part of town. Hot Springs has many handsome sandstone buildings along River Street, including the Fall River County Courthouse and the Hot Springs railway station.

Cross the Fall River, then take a right at Battle Mountain Avenue, named after the battles fought there by the Lakota and Cheyenne for control of the healing waters. The avenue curves northward and becomes Sherman Street. Soon you'll be on your way out of town, passing the Cornerstone Bible Institute and Kemo Sabay Campground. Stay on 385 as it crosses the prairie and enters Wind Cave National Park.

Wind Cave is a sacred place to many Native Americans. When the Sioux arrived, they heard and felt the cold wind rushing out of the cave, and thought a giant lived there. A medicine man visited the cave and a young maiden, the buffalo lady, appeared to him in a vision. She told him to leave offerings in the cave and the Great Spirit would provide vast herds of buffalo for the people to use. Wind Cave became a tourist attraction in the 1890s as whites built a hotel near the entrance and stagecoaches provided rides to the site. Today, Wind Cave is part of the National Park Service and tours are guided by NPS rangers. Tickets are available on a first-come, first-served basis.

At this point, you can remain on 385 and return to Custer via Pringle, or take a right on SD 87 and continue through the park. The pavement is good, and the route involves a number of twisties and a pigtail bridge just north of the park. There are several pullouts along the way where you can stop and take a look at the scenery.

Midway along 87 is the entrance to Custer State Park. The entrance fee is $10 for a motorcycle, and it's good for seven days. You may see buffalo moving freely through the area. It's fun to watch them run (as long as they're not running at you), with their funny, rocking gait.

The road crosses French Creek and makes a U around the Bluebell Lodge and stables, then squiggles its way through the hills past Stockdale Lake. When it meets US 16A, you can go left to Custer, or right toward Mount Rushmore.

Needles Highway

14 miles via SD 87

A.B.A.T.E. Skill Level: Yellow (difficult)

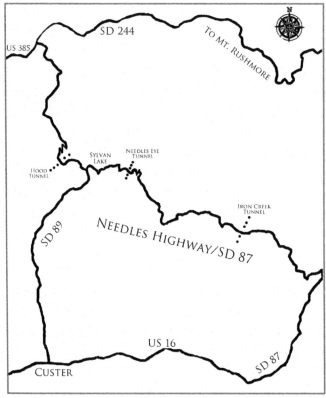

Needles Highway has some of the most spectacular scenery you can ride!

The Needles Highway is short – just 14 miles – but it will test your slow-riding skills with 360 curves, 32 switchbacks and three narrow tunnels. Follow Ralph's advice and stick to the posted speeds; they're low for a reason. If you're in the Black Hills during the Sturgis rally,
be prepared for a long wait to take your turn at the tunnels.

The roadway is named after the needle-like rock formations that surround it. It was conceived by Peter Norbeck, a conservationist and self-styled engineer (he didn't have much time for the "diploma boys") who sought to highlight the grandest views of the Black Hills. Traveling on foot and on horseback, he laid out the route. He achieved his goal through the use of hairpin turns, tunnels, and pigtail bridges. Construction was completed in 1922. Norbeck went on to become South Dakota's governor from 1917 to 1921. He also served in the U.S. Senate. Today, his name is attached to a 66-mile scenic double loop that includes not only the Needles Highway, but Iron Mountain Road, and the Wildlife Loop in Custer State Park.

We rode the Needles Highway on a bright, clear day that promised highs in the 60s, quite a change from our previous day's sojourn through the snow in Spearfish Canyon. We followed US 16A east out of Custer.

The Forest Service had been cleaning up the forest; piles of brush dotted the mountain meadows like muskrat lodges in a bright green swamp. The blacktop furled and unfurled in front of us. Signs here and there warned of S curves. And then we began seeing signs for road construction. It was the second week of May, and I'm sure the South Dakota highway department wanted to make repairs before the tourist season began in earnest.

Traffic was soon restricted to one lane. We waited for several minutes to take our turn at the junction of SD 87 South and 16A.

The road had been stripped down to gravel and signs warned motorcyclists to exercise caution. We slowly made our way over the lumps and bumps and sped up when we came to blacktop again.

We connected with the Needles Highway at the south end of the route, where SD 87 runs concurrently with US 16A, and entered a woodland of towering Ponderosa pines. Five deer appeared at the edge of the road and immediately high-tailed it back into the woods. The road wound through the trees, and we began the climb to the Needles.

In two curves, we were cruising alongside Legion Lake. The water reflected the deep blue sky, and I imagined it must feel pretty good on a hot summer's day. Three deer skittered across the highway as we approached an S-turn. Then 87 split from 16A and we turned left. We stopped at a park building, prepared to pay an entrance fee of some sort, but it was unoccupied, so we traveled onward.

We came to a sign warning of the clearances of the Iron Creek tunnel, the first of three on the route. At 9 feet wide and 12 feet, 3 inches high, it's a tight squeeze for the tourist buses that travel the area. We soon caught up to a little yellow school bus and were forced to poke along behind it as it negotiated the increasingly curvier road.

The bus pulled over before it reached the tunnel, so I dismounted the motorcycle and walked through the hole in the mountain. I waited on the other side as Ralph rode through, hoping to catch a good action shot on my camera. The bus wasn't far behind.

The road changes character beyond the tunnel. The curves become more numerous, and tighter as you gradually gain in elevation. It roughly follows the meanderings of Grace Coolidge Creek, named for the wife of President Calvin Coolidge. (If you like to fly-fish, it's known for yielding fine rainbow trout.) The terrain becomes more rugged, and more curves are needed to skirt the bases of the jagged rocks that protrude sharply out of the earth. There are several pullouts along the way if you want to stop and take pictures or let an impatient driver pass you.

The Needles are awesome from any angle.

This is the oldest part of the Black Hills, the oldest mountain range in North America. The mountains are remnants of a mountainous dome that has been eroded by wind and weather for an estimated 2 billion years.

A pair of hairpin turns brings you to the Cathedral Spires trailhead. A small parking lot allows you to get off your bike and hike the 1.6-mile trail, or just relax and take in the stunning views. The jagged peaks surround the road, which is quite steep.

The highway continues to twist and climb to the Needles Eye tunnel. The Needles Eye is a natural rock formation created by wind, rain, and freezing and thawing ice. The tunnel is man-made, blasted out of the rock with dynamite to an opening 8 feet, 4 inches wide by 12 feet tall. It's the smallest of the three tunnels on SD 87. The school bus had passed us at the Iron Creek tunnel. We watched as it slowly inched its way ahead of us through the rocky tube of the Needles Eye. Ralph followed close behind.

We spent a few minutes resting in the parking lot/pullout on the north side of the tunnel, then got back on the road before the bus and its load of kids could slow us down. SD 87 curled up to the shores of Sylvan Lake, then began to lose elevation shortly after we passed the Sylvan Lake Lodge. After a few moderate curves, we came to the Hood tunnel. At 10 feet, 6 inches wide and 10 feet, 7 inches high, it's almost square.

A series of four hairpin turns followed the tunnel and hastened the decline in elevation. The highway made longer, sweeping turns as it passed through Johnson Canyon and past the Horse Thief Campgrounds. A few more sweepers brought us to US 385/US 16.

SD 244

12 miles

A.B.A.T.E. Skill Level: Red (somewhat challenging)

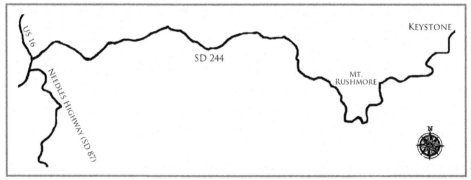

SD244 leads directly to Mount Rushmore.

This is a short ride, but it gives you a different perspective on Mount Rushmore. To reach it from the Needles Highway, take a short (half-mile) cruise on US 16/US 385, then take a right onto SD 244.

Alternatively, you can ride south out of Hill City (244 is concurrent with US 385 here), past the Silver Dollar Saloon, until 244 splits from US 16/US 385. Take a left.

The only highway that runs directly to Mount Rushmore, SD 244 is also known as Borglum Memorial Highway, named after Gutzon Borglum, the sculptor of Mount Rushmore. It was once part of the Needles Highway, and is part of the Peter Norbeck Scenic Byway.

View George Washington from a different angle on SD 244.

The change from the almost freeway-like federal highway to the two-lane state highway is dramatic. You will immediately encounter a series of wide, sweeping curves as you head east through the Black Hills National Forest. After a couple of miles, the road begins to head southeast. It gets curvier as you swoop through the hills. The forest surrounds you, and the air is fresh and clean.

About two-thirds of the way to Mount Rushmore, the road skims by Horse Thief Lake, then makes some long, almost square corners. Keep a lookout for mountain goats, and tourists stopping to look at mountain goats. Be on the lookout, too, for patrol cars. The area is an infamous speed trap.

The curves become tighter as you near the national monument. Just before you reach Mount Rushmore, you'll come to a pullout. It's worth a stop here to take a picture of the mountains opposite the parking lot. You'll see George Washington's profile, a somewhat different look at the monument than the full-on view usually presented in tourist brochures.

Continue on past the pullout. The road curves directly into the Mount Rushmore National Monument gates, and you'll see George, Thomas, Teddy and Abe in all their glory. Motorcycle parking at the monument was $11 when we visited; admission to the monument is free.

You could easily spend a day at Mount Rushmore, learning how Borglum and Italian sculptor Luigi Del Bianco sculpted the presidents' faces and the story of how the mountain came to be carved. It's especially inspiring to visit the monument at night as the sun sets and the faces are lit. The Park Service puts on an excellent multi-media show. If you don't come away feeling patriotic and teary-eyed, you don't have a soul.

North Playhouse Road to US 16A

7 miles
A.B.A.T.E. Skill Level: Black (easy)

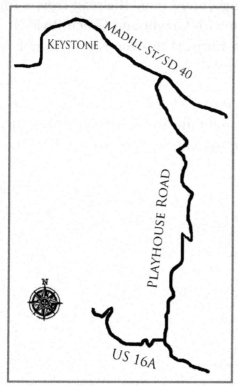

Playhouse Road is a great way
to avoid congestion in Keystone!

If you don't want to drive through the tourist trap known as Keystone (it's like the midway at a state fair), the Playhouse Road is a fun ride that neatly misses all the downtown traffic. As you come into Keystone off of Iron Mountain Road, cruise past the National Presidential Wax Museum, Rushmore Borglum Story, the Rushmore Mountain Taffy Shop, and the Keystone Station for the 1880 Train. Take a left onto Madill Street (SD 40). This will lead you out of town and into the countryside very quickly, although there are plenty of restaurants, bars, and motels along the way.

A bridge crosses Battle Creek just before you get to Playhouse Road. Slow down and take a right. Playhouse Road immediately takes you into a curling ride through the forest. It's pleasant, with nice curves and a switchback to make things interesting. The road crosses Iron Creek just after its intersection with Greyhound Gulch Road. It makes a pair of almost-hairpin turns, then swoops by a number of ranches before meeting up with US 16A.

Playhouse Road continues on into Custer State Park. The Black Hills Playhouse is in the park and puts on theatrical performances, including Broadway plays, throughout the summer.

Iron Mountain Road

17 miles via US 16A
A.B.A.T.E. Skill Level: Yellow (difficult)

Iron Mountain Road packs in a lot of exciting riding in just 17 miles.

If your need is for speed, Iron Mountain Road is probably not for you. If, however, you're looking for a road with character, check this out:

- 314 curves
- 14 switchbacks
- 3 pigtail bridges
- 3 one-lane tunnels
- 2 splits
- 4 presidents*

Throw in a spectacular view of Mount Rushmore at the 5,445-foot summit, and you have a complete package. Whether you start at the top, near Keystone, and ride down, or begin in Custer State Park and ride up, Iron Mountain Road is one heckuva ride!

You will see several signs warning motorcyclists especially to adhere to the speed limit, which at times can be as low as 15 mph. Heed them! We encountered sprays of rock on the road, and an occasional bowling-ball sized chunk of limestone or granite that could easily turn your world upside down if you're not paying attention.

Riding south from Keystone, the road very quickly begins its twisting journey to the top. In a couple of quick turns, you'll reach a small bridge that crosses Grizzly Bear Creek. Less than a mile later, you'll encounter the first pigtail bridge.

The pigtail bridges were designed by Cecil C. Gideon, who also designed the State Game Lodge in Custer State Park. The wooden bridges are designed to take you safely through quick changes in elevation without destroying the natural beauty of the surrounding Black Hills. They also slow you down (the top speed on Iron Mountain Road is 35 mph and the bridges slow you down to about 15). Again, they're a test of your slow-driving skills.

The second pigtail bridge is no more than a mile from the first. It's followed by a split in the highway that was designed to disturb the landscape as little as possible. The split briefly transforms the two-lane road to a pair of side-by-side, one-lane, one-way streets that take you on a little side trip through the forest before you come to the third pigtail bridge. It's fun to look down and see the road you just rode below you.

Approaching the Doane Robinson Tunnel

A couple of twists up the mountainside brings you to another split. The one-lanes are a little farther apart here; they continue until you reach the turnoff for the Iron Mountain Picnic Area. A parking lot is just three turns away. It's a good place to stop for photos; the view is panoramic.

Below the parking lot, a series of switchbacks starts to bring you down to a lower elevation and the Doane Robinson tunnel. It's named after the man who conceived the idea of Mount Rushmore and introduced a bill in the South Dakota legislature to authorize carving a mountain in Custer State Park. (Permission was granted, but no funding was approved.) The tunnel, 14 feet wide and 12 feet, 9 inches high, was designed to frame a view of Mount Rushmore as you drive through it from the south. Signs warn of falling rock and ask you to sound your horn to let others know you're coming. A break in the roof of the tunnel allows a shaft of sunlight in. It's like two tunnels in one! The road was widened a bit here in 2015, and a decorative guardrail was put up at a cost of $3.4 million.

A series of small sweepers leads to the C.C. Gideon tunnel. It's 13 feet, 2 inches wide and 12 feet, 2 inches high. The third tunnel is named after Scovel Johnson, the man who actually graded the road and blasted the tunnels to create the Needles Highway. He also made the preliminary surveys of the Iron Mountain Road. His tunnel is 13 feet, 4 inches wide by 12 feet, 4 inches high. Both tunnels frame Mount Rushmore; when you come up from the south, they give you your first glimpse of the monument.

The road continues to snake through the hills, winding past resorts and campgrounds and generally following along Spokane Creek. The terrain becomes less mountainous as you continue riding south. The prairie comes into view, and it's time to keep a lookout for buffalo. The road retains its meandering curves, however, all the way up to its junction with SD 36. The two highways run concurrently up to the entrance of Custer State Park and the Peter Norbeck Visitor Center.

Wildlife Loop Road, Custer State Park

18 miles
A.B.A.T.E. Skill Level: Red (somewhat challenging)

It's a slow ride on the Wildelife Loop.

Though A.B.A.T.E. rates this road as "somewhat challenging", the biggest challenge you'll most likely run into is getting around the tourists!

We entered the park at the north end, where we paid the $10 entrance fee and received a little tag to put on the motorcycle that enabled us to make as many visits to the park as we wanted for the next seven days.

The road takes several sweeping curves as it cuts south through the rolling prairie. In early May, the prairie grasses were a bright emerald green, which made the Ponderosa Pines on the hills seem even darker.

The park was established as a wildlife reserve in 1913 and was named Custer State Park in 1919. It was named after Lieutenant Colonel George Armstrong Custer, who led a scientific army expedition into the Black Hills in 1874. Its 71,000 square acres are home to bison, elk, mule deer, white tail deer, mountain goats, pronghorn, mountain lions, feral burros, coyotes, and a critter that looks like a giant (raccoon-sized) orange squirrel – the yellow-bellied marmot. We saw a couple of them in the park. When I asked the folks at the EconoLodge in Custer about it, they tried to pass it off as a jackalope, the mythical jack rabbit with a set of deer antlers, but I set them straight. "You only see those in bars," I said, "or in Wall Drug."

Like all of the roads in the Black Hills, the Wildlife Loop is well maintained. We did encounter sand in some places, and occasional buffalo chips. More than 1,300 bison roam the park freely – this is their land – and they go where they want to (literally). Signs throughout the park warn you, "Do Not Approach the Buffalo."

As we meandered through the park, grazing pronghorn occasionally popped up their heads to look at the noisy beast running by them. (Ralph added true dual ceramic-coated pipes to the Victory to improve performance, and they're loud!) Pronghorns, also called antelope, are the fastest land animal in North America and can hit speeds of 60 mph. They're handsome animals with tan-and-white striped coats and black noses. Unlike true antelope, they shed their horns every year.

The road makes an arc around Custer State Park Airport. The airport is open to general aviation and averages about 30 visitors per month. Pilots, too, have to keep an eye out for wildlife. South of the airport, the curves a little more numerous and tighter, but you won't encounter any switchbacks here.

The buffalo corrals are at the southern end of the loop. Every September, on the last Friday of the month, the state rounds up the buffalo and herds them into the corrals for sorting, testing and branding. A herd of 36 was introduced to the park in 1914, when the shaggy mammals had been hunted nearly into extinction. By 1940, the herd had grown to more than 2,500, and the animals were over-grazing the park. The roundup is a way to keep the herd healthy, and private citizens volunteer to mount their horses and bring the ornery beasts in.

Feral burros cause a traffic jam in Custer State Park.

A two-day art festival precedes the event, and a pancake-and-sausage breakfast kicks off the morning. Visitors are asked to stay in the viewing areas until all the bison have entered the corrals. For more information, visit **http://gfp.sd.gov/state-parks/directory/custer/events/buffalo-roundup.**

The corrals are near a favorite hangout of the feral burros. Years ago, they were used to haul tourists to the top of Harney Peak, the tallest mountain in the Black Hills (7,242 feet above sea level). They were set free when the service was discontinued, and their descendants have roamed the hills ever since. They are notorious beggars and will stick their heads into cars for carrots, apples, and anything else they can scrounge. Traffic along the loop can back up for nearly a mile when they come down the road. They don't like it when a motorcycle "snorts" at them, however, and will move out of the way. (Which is more than can be said for the tourists in the cars.)

Past the corrals, the road starts bending back to the north. Now and then, a car full of tourists would pull over and people would emerge to view a distant buffalo herd.

When we neared the Prairie Dog Town, the little rodents popped out of their burrows and chattered at us, their little black tails sticking up like flags. Though they're cute and fun to watch, you don't want to get too close. They harbor bubonic plague!

As we angled slowly up toward SD 87, we encountered a small group of buffalo running across the road and down a hill. It was mid-afternoon, and they were moving from one grazing area to another. Little orange-brown calves just a few days old scampered alongside their mothers and scruffy-looking bulls.

We rode a few yards further down the road and another group came running toward us and dashed down the same hill. Clearly, this was a daily bison migration path. It was a thrill to see them run, although a little nerve-wracking when they were coming straight at us.

Keep a safe distance from buffalo.

We came upon a third group just a few more yards down the road. The leader stopped and stared at us. Buffalo will charge for any reason or no reason at all. They can wheel and spin and charge faster than you would think a 2,000-lb. animal can move. And more than one motorcyclist has reported that they seem to like to charge bikes with loud pipes.

We scarcely dared to breathe. Slowly, cautiously, Ralph backed the bike away from the herd. The leader continued to stare at us, decided we weren't going to challenge his authority. He turned his back on us and pushed his followers up the hill and away from the road.

Relaxing a bit, we continued our way around the park. As we neared a relatively open area, we came upon a parked car. Its occupants had gotten out and were approaching a large bison resting alongside the road. We got the hell out of there.

Deerfield Road

18 miles
A.B.A.T.E. Skill Level: Red (somewhat challenging)

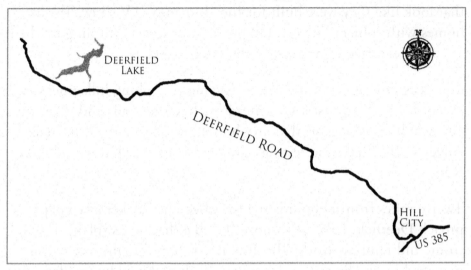

Deerfield Road is a pleasant ride to nowhere.

Deerfield Road out of Hill City doesn't have the tight curves found on other Black Hills roads. There's something else it doesn't have much of – traffic. We set out on this meandering ride in late afternoon, trying to make maximum use of the still-early spring daylight.

Deerfield Road starts out as Harney Peak West Road leading off of US 385 near the Museum of the Black Hills in Hill City. Within a couple of blocks, it becomes a road in its own right and stretches westward through the hills.

Within a mile, you'll come to Wade's Gold Mill, a family-owned museum dedicated to gold mining. Stop in on your way back to Hill City and pan for gold if you've a mind to. Wade's Mill is open from 9 a.m. to 6 p.m. from Memorial Day to Labor Day. Adult admission is $18 and includes a tour and a gold-panning lesson.

After Wade's Mill, the road makes a big arc near a trailer park next to Newton Fork, then settles into a regular rhythm of curves. Slow down for the occasional metal cattle guard running cross-wise across the road. As you travel along the Deerfield Road, you'll see ranches that look like they were built for the "Bonanza" TV show. The log homes with split-rail fences, tall pines, and streams running by them are picture-perfect, quintessential western ranches.

The trees thin out in some places, leaving the rolling hills uncovered except for tough grasses. Hay meadows line the roads and occasionally, you'll cross streams that are shunted under the road through culverts. They have interesting names such as Slate Creek and Gold Run.

Twelve miles from Hill City, the trees become thicker as you approach Deerfield Lake. It's a no-wake lake that holds splake, brook trout, and rainbow trout. The 400-acre lake is actually a reservoir managed by the Bureau of Reclamation. It's formed by the dam at the western end, where Castle Creek flows in and out. The water is deep blue, tinged with aquamarine. There are three campgrounds around the lake.

A mile or so past the reservoir, the blacktop ends at a Y. The fork on the left is West Deerfield Road, and this gravel road can take you into Wyoming, where it becomes Castle Creek Road. The fork on the right is the South Rochford Road, which, at this writing, is undergoing ecological assessment for road improvements.

Vanoker Canyon Road (Sturgis to Nemo)

17 miles
A.B.A.T.E. Skill Level: Orange (somewhat difficult)

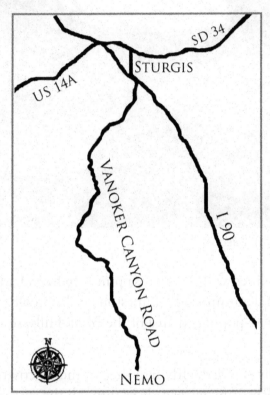

Vanoker Canyon Road provides a more relaxing ride.

Vanoker Canyon Road isn't as curlicued as Iron Mountain Road, but it has some turns and tricks to keep you awake. One week after our visit, three people were hurt in motorcycle wrecks after they missed a curve.

You can pick it up on the east side of Sturgis on Junction Ave. Ride south out of town, past the Belle Joli Winery. The road begins twisting and turning within a mile. Although you can ride a little faster on this road than some others, the curves can be deceiving. Ralph was able to steer the course with a minimal amount of shifting.

Vanoker Canyon Road is lightly traveled.

The two-lane highway is lined with Ponderosa pine, birch, and aspen, which makes for a colorful autumn ride. Limestone walls provide dramatic views. It's in a less-populated area of the Black Hills, so you don't feel crowded.

Vanoker Canyon is lightly traveled, although there is more activity during the Sturgis rally. The canyon road slices through the surrounding hills and weaves its way around ranches. It parallels Meadow Creek for a good way before veering southeast. Smaller gravel roads feed into it and you'll see driveway aprons that lead to nowhere.

About halfway down the route, you'll see signs for Wonderland Cave on Alpine Road, which is gravel. The cave has more than two dozen rooms; the first commercial tours began in the 1930s. The cave is open seven days a week from 8 a.m. to 7 p.m. during the summer.

As the road nears Nemo, the trees give way to hayfields. The road dead-ends at Nemo Road.

Nemo to Johnson Siding via Nemo Road and Norris Peak Road

12 miles
A.B.A.T.E. Skill Level: Orange (somewhat difficult) and Yellow (difficult)

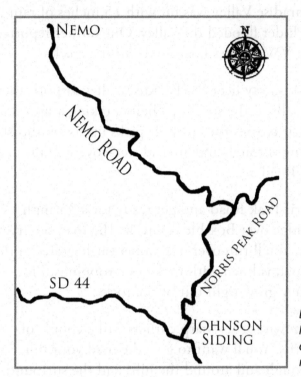

Be careful driving Norris Peak Road, one of the Black Hills' most dangerous.

It's just a short ride into Nemo from the intersection of Vanoker Canyon Road and Nemo Road. It's a tiny place, with a population of just over 500 people. It was established in 1877as a lumber camp to serve the gold mines near Lead.

The road curves through Nemo, past the Nemo Schoolhouse. The school was built in the 1920s and continued to serve area children into the 1980s, when decreased enrollment dictated that they receive their education in Lead. The building, which is on the South Dakota and National Historic Register, is now a hotel. Some of the rooms share the Boys' and Girls' bathrooms.

The Nemo Mercantile is nearby, and Big Mama's Beer Garden is just down the road.

Leaving Nemo, the road loosely follows the meandering Box Elder Creek. In 1972, the Paradise Valley was hit with 15 inches of rain in six hours and the Box Elder flooded the valley. One farmer reported seeing rocks the size of VW Beetles floating down the creek.

There's a bit of a straight-away near the Paradise Valley airport, then road runs up over the hills to the southeast before taking a near U-turn to the north as it crosses the creek. It picks up its southeastern route again, winding through and around tree-covered hills until it Ys with Norris Peak Road.

Take a right onto Norris Peak Road and get ready for a 35-mph curve that crosses a bridge over Box Elder Creek. The road S-curves between some ranches. You'll run over occasional cattle grates in this area. Further on, the road is lined with rocky outcroppings. Pine trees look as though they grow right out of the rocks.

Norris Peak Road is known for its sharp corners and a couple of hair-raising hairpin turns. You'll want to give the road your full attention as it cuts through and around the hills and the surrounding forest. The curves are near-continuous. The shoulders are narrow to non-existent. Signs warn of a steep downgrade, then a 15-mph curve.

The curves become sharper and more numerous as you approach the bridge over Rapid Creek.

Two reverse curves were straightened out in 2016, to cut down on motorcycle accidents about three-quarters of a mile from Johnson Siding. The road was widened a bit and guardrails were installed. It makes a safer ride into town, and to the intersection with SD 44.

Chapter 3

The Badlands

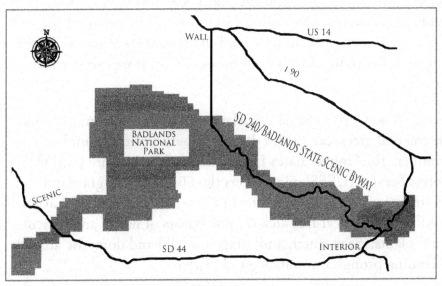

Follow the Badlands Loop Scenic Byway to some weird and wonderful places.

Stark. Incredibly silent. Hot during the day, cold at night. A place so forbidding even the Lakota called it "mako sika" – land bad.

A trip to the Black Hills is not complete until you've visited the Badlands, 244,000 acres of rugged lunar landscape that protrudes from the surrounding prairie. Though reminiscent of the Desert Southwest, the Badlands have their own distinct geology and character.

The rock formations in the Badlands are layers of rock laid down some 70 million years ago. About 500,000 years ago, the Cheyenne River flooded the area, and erosion began to do its work. Since then, the Badlands have lost about an inch a year to wind and weather. They're expected to disappear completely in another 500,000 years.

We approached the Badlands from the west on SD 44. The contrast between the Black Hills and the prairie couldn't have been more apparent. Deciduous trees replaced evergreens. The morning sun was bright, the sky a brilliant blue, and the road surface was well-used but smooth. Traffic was light to non-existent. It was an excellent day to ride.

The Buffalo Gap National Grassland spread out in front of us like an emerald green carpet. It's decorated with flowers in mid-to-late summer. The United States Department of Agriculture (USDA)'s Forest Service (USFS) administers the 600,000-acre grassland. It's an important ecosystem of intact prairie that provides habitat for wildlife, a chemical-free area for pollinators of native and agricultural plants, clean water, and forage for wild and domestic animals including pronghorn, buffalo, and cattle.

About midway between Farmingdale and Scenic, near the Cheyenne River, we saw a large dinosaur statue standing in a field all by itself. There were no signs pointing to it. I thought maybe a local farmer had acquired an old Sinclair Oil dino and placed it there to amuse himself.

It turned out to be the last remnant of a town called Creston. The Milwaukee Railroad used to stop there to take on water for its steam engines during the gold rush days. The dinosaur was built in 1933 by Emmet A. Sullivan, and is thought to be the earliest roadside dino every built. It was made with scrap metal and concrete and pointed the way to the Creston General Store. Students from the South Dakota School of Mines and Technology restored the statute in the late '90s. Sullivan, by the way, also designed the dinosaurs in

Dinosaur Park in Rapid City, and the brontosaurus at Wall Drug.

Intent on getting to the Badlands Loop Road, we didn't stop in Scenic, a ghost town now owned by the Iglesia ni Cristo Church, a Filipino Church of Christ. I wish we had. It would have been fun to poke around the abandoned saloon and jail. By the way, there is a working gas station there.

As we drew nearer to the Badlands, we began to see little tables of rock pushing their way up through the prairie.

The road made lazy, sweeping curves. The scenery began to take on a more "mountainous" look as the Badlands came into view. We swept past Imlay, a town that was abandoned during the Dust Bowl of the 1930s. A grove of trees is pretty much all that's left.

The road straightened out and the mountains seemed tantalizingly out of reach. Buttes appeared alongside of us on the right and the mountains that had been before us slid off to the left. There was land and there was sky. We passed the road to Bouquet Table. The mesa looked like a miniature version of Ayer's Rock in Australia.

Coming up to the Conata Road, the highway sign pointed left to SD 240, the Badlands Loop Road. The story now becomes a case of "don't do as we did, do as we tell you." Instead of riding eleven miles on 44 to Interior and catching the Loop there, we took a left.

The Conata Road is dirt. Soft dirt. The back end of the Victory fishtailed on the powdery surface and I thought we might drop the bike. I began to question my husband's sanity. What would we do if we went down or ran out of gas on this Godforsaken road? I imagined buzzards picking over our lifeless carcasses.

The road ran due north without curves. We passed over a cattle guard and continued onward. As we neared the Badlands, little rock tables pushed their way out of the ground. We crossed another cattle guard. Ralph drove resolutely toward the mountains and I sat on the back of the bike and fretted. We came to a third cattle guard – and pavement! Within a mile, we were in the heart of the Badlands.

Though they're difficult to see in black and white, the Badlands formations have stripes of many colors.

The road climbed upward and the banded rock formations stood out against the blazing blue sky. Gray, tan, yellow, pink, and green stripes – all different layers of ancient sediment – contrasted vividly with the green grass at the bases of the mounds. After coming

GPS may work in the Badlands, but your cell phone won't.

through the dirt, we felt triumphant. We stopped to take pictures and marvel at the scenery.

The road curled forward until it reached a T, the Badlands Loop Road. We took a left and followed SD 240 as it carved its way through the hills. We passed the Ancient Hunters Overlook where Native Americans drove bison over the edge to their deaths. There's a small parking lot there if you want to look out over the scene.

The road made a couple of wide U-turns and some wide, sweeping turns before heading straight north out of the park. We waited our turn at the Pinnacles entrance/exit, then resumed riding north on 240 to Wall.

If You Go

The route: *Take SD 240 from I 90 or from Interior. Don't follow our path!*

Lodging: *Cedar Pass Lodge is the only the place to stay inside Badlands National Park. The lodge consists of twelve cabins built to LEED standards and placed in the park during 2012-2013. The Badlands Inn is just outside the park in Interior. Reservations are a must during the tourist season. Visit http://www. cedarpasslodge.com/lodging.*

If you like to camp, the fourteen campsites at Cedar Pass Camp Grounds are just $10 per campsite per night. Group campsites are available, and all campsites are first-come, first-served. Fires are not allowed in the Badlands, but you can use camp stoves.

Gas stations: *There are gas stations outside the park at Cactus Flat, Rapid City, Interior, Scenic, Kadoka, Wanblee, Philip, and Wall.*

Cell Phone Service: *Cell phones will not work in most of the park.*

Entrance Fees: *$10 gets you a seven-day motorcycle pass.*

Weather: *Severe thunderstorms are common during the summer, and temperatures easily reach 100 degrees.*

Speed limit: 45 mph

Chapter 4

Things to See and Do in the Black Hills

To Native Americans, the Black Hills, paha sapa, were the center of the earth. It was where life began and where they began. Reverence for the area remains strong.

It's easy to see why. With its hills covered with towering Ponderosa pine and mountain meadows filled with wildlife, these mountains must have been paradise. Though the hills are dotted now with cities instead of tipis, they remain incredibly beautiful.

The cities themselves offer quite a bit in the way of entertainment, from 24/7 gambling in Deadwood to the motorcycle museum in Sturgis.

Custer

Custer City is in the center of the Black Hills, and we made it our base of operations while we researched this book.

Custer is named after Lt. Colonel George Armstrong Custer, who camped here in 1874 while exploring the Black Hills. A member of his party discovered gold on French Creek, and the Black Hills were forever changed. As prospectors moved in, the Lakota were pushed out of their sacred lands. The Indians killed Custer at the Battle of the Little Big Horn in Montana two years later. They're still fighting (through the courts) for their land.

Custer has a number of eating establishments. One of our favorites is **Bitter Esters Brewhouse**. The little brew pub specializes in English and Belgian-style ales and sausages. I ordered the Ranchers

Custer Museum

Pie (the South Dakota version of shepherd's pie), and it was marvelous comfort food after a cold, snowy day in Spearfish Canyon. Another is the **Buglin' Bull Restaurant and Sports Bar** just down the street. The bison burgers were delicious. Ralph tried the Custer Armstrong ale and liked it well enough to bring home a souvenir glass.

The State Game Lodge Dining Room in Custer State Park serves South Dakota pheasant, buffalo, and trout.

If you're up for some wine tasting, stop in at the **Naked Winery Tasting Room**. The wines are made in Oregon, but the fun is in South

Dakota! Of special interest to bikers is their Outdoor Vino, which comes in a BPA-free plastic bottle that fits nicely in a saddlebag. You don't have to worry about it breaking, so you can bring some home as gift for your dog sitter. There are Naked Winery Tasting Rooms in Hill City and Keystone, too.

The National Museum of Woodcarving is on the west side of town. The work of more than 70 carvers is displayed there. It's a great place to hang out on a rainy day.

Somewhat overlooked is the **1881 Courthouse Museum**. Housed in the former Dakota Territory courthouse, the museum features artifacts from Custer's expedition, a taxidermy display that includes an extinct species of mountain sheep that's been studied by the Smithsonian Institution, a mining exhibit, and pioneer clothing and furniture. Out in back is a stable full of old carriages and cars.

Deadwood

Downtown Deadwood was nearly deserted on a snowy/rainy day. Deadwood has been a city full of characters and fun ever since it sprang to life in 1876 during the Black Hills Gold Rush. With Wild Bill Hickok, Calamity Jane, Colorado Charley Utter, Madam Mustache, and Dirty Em walking the streets, how could it be anything but?

But the dusty, historic Deadwood I remember from childhood is slicked up now with casinos and fancy hotels on nearly every block. There's even a Starbucks! In 1989, South Dakota voters allowed limited stakes gambling in the city, which allowed Deadwood to preserve and reconstruct many of its historic buildings. The cobblestone streets in the center of town reflect late nineteenth century charm.

Downtown Deadwood was nearly deserted on a snowy/rainy day.

Cadillac Jack's, the **Tin Lizzie,** the **Wooden Nickel** and the **Celebrity Hotel and Casino** are just a few of the gambling establishments you'll find in Deadwood.

If gambling is not your thing, you can visit the **Adams Museum, Days of '76 Museum, Historic Adams House, or the Homestake Adams Research and Cultural Center,** located downtown. Just north of Deadwood is **Tatanka,** actor Kevin Costner's tribute to bison and the culture of the American Indian. And you can still see daily shootouts on Main Street, except during the Sturgis rally.

Deadwood Harley-Davidson sells only H-D clothing and accessories.

Hill City

There's a lot going on in Hill City. One of the most-visited attractions near the town is the **Crazy Horse Memorial**, just off of US 385, about half-way between Custer and Hill City. Carving on the memorial began in 1948; survivors of the Battle of the Little Big Horn attended the first blast. The project is privately funded, so progress has been slow. A museum and restaurant and gift shop are on the grounds. A laser show is projected onto the memorial every evening from May to September.

Also in Hill City is the **Prairie Berry Winery**, a family-owned winery making wines based on a grandmother's recipes. Its Red Ass Rhubarb wine is a bestseller, and its Black Raspberry Merlot Fusion won a double gold medal at the 2016 Tasters Guild International Wine Competition. Next to Prairie Berry is the **Miner Brewing Company**, owned by the same family.

We had great food at **Desperados**, which was one of two restaurants recommended to us by the Hill City Visitor Information Center. I had the fresh salmon sandwich, and it was a nice change from all the beef you typically find on a South Dakota menu. Also recommended was the **Alpine Inn**.

Hill City has lots of shops. One in particular had some very interesting Native American art. It's probably a good thing that we didn't look past the front window. There was no room for it on the motorcycle. The Harley-Davidson shop in Hill City sells H-D merchandise, but no bikes.

Hot Springs

Located on the southern end of the Black Hills, Hot Springs has a quaint downtown that invites exploration. The two key attractions are the **Mammoth Site** (described on page 40), and the **Evans Plunge**. The plunge is the oldest tourist attraction in the Black Hills, founded in 1890. Five thousand gallons of natural spring water flows from a thermal spring at the north end of the pool. This is the hot spring the Indians fought over. The water is an inviting 86 degrees. The plunge is owned and operated by the city of Hot Springs and is open from 6 a.m. to 8 p.m. Monday through Friday and 10 a.m. to 8 p.m. Saturday and Sunday throughout the summer.

Mount Rushmore still inspires.

Keystone

The main reason to visit Keystone is to see **Mount Rushmore**. Another would be to ride the 1880 Train from Keystone to Hill City and back. Privately owned, the Black Hills Central Railroad operates two restored steam engines that shuttle railcars between the two cities. The train runs May through December. Visit **https://www.1880train.com for more information**.

Spearfish

Spearfish Creek runs through downtown Spearfish. Spearfish is a town for people who love the outdoors. Hiking, fishing, and mountain biking are big here.

If you need to spend a day indoors, try the **Termesphere Gallery**. Artist Dick Termes paints on spheres, suspends them from the ceiling and rotates them slowly to create a complete world or environment in a ball. Another place to consider is the **High Plains Western Heritage Center** that showcases Native American lore, cowboy lore, and the mining and forestry industries.

Spearfish has many restaurants. We tried **Killian's Tavern**. We were trying to decide whether to go there or the bar next door when a couple of young men came out. "How's the food?" I asked. "Fantastic!" one of them replied. "How's the beer?" "Even better!" Killian's serves locally-grown foods and locally-brewed beer from Spearfish's own **Crow Peak Brewery**, which is open 11 a.m. to 10 p.m. Monday through Thursday, Friday and Saturday from 11 a.m. to 12 a.m., and 11 a.m. to 9 p.m. Sunday.

Outdoor Motorsports sells Hondas, Can-Ams, and Ural sidecars.

Sturgis

Sturgis is a biker's town from start to finish. Even when the rally isn't happening, it caters to bikers.

The first place to visit is the **Sturgis Motorcycle Museum and Hall of Fame**. Housed in the former post office, the museum has big expansion plans – one day, a giant motorcycle will protrude from the main entrance. Until then, however, you can take a look at a Harley-Davidson made for the fiftieth anniversary of the Sturgis rally, a beautiful creamy white bike with solid gold trim. Also on hand are several Excelsior Hendersons, including a brand-new, in-the-shipping-crate model from the 1990s attempt at a manufacturing restart, a 1909 Imperial, and a hand-carved wooden Harley. Admission is $8.50 for adults.

After touring the museum, we strolled across the street to **Hot Leathers**. Ralph had misplaced his chaps along the way and despite his wind/rain suit, he felt the cold. The saleswoman helped him buy and fit new chaps. My feet were cold, so I picked up an extra pair of socks. She pulled out a step-stool for me to sit on while I put them on. I said, "I think bikers are the nicest people in the world." She agreed. "They're much nicer than the Corvette people who come here. And the cowboys…" she rolled her eyes.

On her advice, we ate lunch at the **Knuckle Saloon**. The staff was attentive and the food was good. The Knuckle is home to Sturgis' first craft brewery and radio station KNKL, "The Voice of Sturgis."

Loud American Roadhouse was also recommended. Of course, Sturgis has no shortage of biker bars, from the **Iron Horse Saloon**, with its multiple stages to **One-Eyed Jack's**. The **Full Throttle Saloon**, the self-proclaimed world's largest biker bar, burned to the ground in late 2015 and has not yet been rebuilt, although the campground is still in operation.

Sturgis Museum

If you need repairs to your bike, or want to buy a new one, there are several motorcycle dealers in town, including **Indian** and **Sturgis Motorsports**, a BMW dealer. The **Harley-Davidson** store in Sturgis sells only clothing and accessories.

Harley-Davidson of the Black Hills is located in Rapid City, and that's where the bikes are. **Deluxe Harley-Davison** has dealerships in Sundance and Gillette, Wyoming.

It's fun to watch a bus maneuver through the tunnels on Needles Highway or Iron Mountain Road.

Fun Facts About the Black Hills

- *The Black Hills cover 8,426 square miles.*

- *The tallest peak is Harney Peak, 7,242 feet above sea level. It is the highest point east of the Rocky Mountains.*

- *The 1.2-million-acre Black Hills National Forest surrounds the city of Custer.*

- *More than 170 miles of Jewel Cave have been mapped; it is the third-largest cave system in the world.*

- *The Black Hills have been inhabited by Native Americans for nearly 10,000 years. The Arikara arrived in the 1500s, followed by the Cheyenne, Crow, Kiowa and Pawnee. The Lakota are latecomers; they arrived in the 1700s.*

- *Gold was discovered in 1874.*

- *The Black Hills are an isolated mountain range, and run east to west instead of north to south like the Rockies or the Appalachians.*

- *The Lakota called them paha sapa, "the hills that are black". The Ponderosa pines that cover the mountain slopes are so dark they look almost black.*

- *Devils Tower in Wyoming is considered part of the Black Hills.*

- *Within the Black Hills are six national parks, more than 1,300 miles of streams, and more than 450 miles of hiking and biking trails.*

More Fun Facts

- The Black Hills are in the Mountain time zone.

- The opening under Crazy Horse's arm is large enough to contain a ten-story building.

- Thomas Jefferson was originally carved to the right of George Washington on Mount Rushmore. That didn't work, so his face was dynamited off and he was placed on George's left.

- An entire city block in Deadwood was occupied by brothels until 1980.

About the Author

Ride the Black Hills is Cynthia Sowden's third motorcycle travel book. Although they got into motorcycles just ten years ago, Sowden and her husband, Ralph, have ridden their 2002 Victory Deluxe Touring Cruiser along Rte. 66 to the Grand Canyon, followed the Mississippi River from its source to New Orleans, and ridden all over Minnesota. They made their trip to the Black Hills in the spring of 2016.

Cynthia is a graduate of the University of Minnesota School of Journalism and Mass Communications. She worked in corporate communications, advertising, and public relations for more than 30 years. Ralph is an electrical engineer, working in the semi-conductor industry. They both look forward to spending more time riding when they retire.

Our Victory turned over 50,000 miles on this trip.

Other Books by
Cynthia Lueck Sowden

Ride Lake Superior (2015, Homegrown Communications)

An Anniversary to Remember (2014, Homegrown Communications)

Ride Minnesota (2013, Homegrown Communications)

Wedding Occasions: 101 New Party Themes for Wedding Showers, Rehearsal Dinners, Engagement Parties and More! (1990, Brighton Publications)

To order personalized copies, visit **www.homegrowncommunications.biz**, or email the author: Cynthia.sowden@gmail.com.

Lightning Source UK Ltd.
Milton Keynes UK
UKOW06f0203010817
306411UK00011B/833/P